THE COLOR BOOK
CADENCE
VOLUME 1

WRITTEN BY
C. J. HENRY

DEDICATION

To my great-grandmother, Laura Henry, Grandmother Laura–Henry Kennerson, and Margaret Anna Jenkins, who is now a Smith, this piece is inspired by you all. Thank you for carrying our families, for being our angels, strength, teachers, and foundation. You have all inspired me and lived through me in many ways internally. Thank you for showing me what life is about.

True colors? Oh, they're there!

TABLE OF CONTENTS

"...I'm a visionary that's long-term."

- Logic

AFFIRMATIVE

Overachieve, I don't under receive.
In me, I believe, a legend conceived.
No need to compare, no space is there,
No need to stare.
Standing tall in the distance as the noblest there.
Those spaces are like ripples in time with tears.
Don't you understand?

Many are Called.
Few are chosen.

Step up to the plate; it's never too late to be great.
It may not register at first.
Nevertheless, what a bigger picture;
much more is at stake.

Just know, there'll be no more than you can take,
No more than you can digest on your plate.
I promise I'm not being facetious,
But even as time passes, you might even remember the
taste.

I die Daily! I eat daily! I shine!
Off-season and on.
I shine like Abra Stone.

It's a choice!
Quiet?
Oh No.
On these toes! There's ten of those.
Against the odds, I lifted my voice.
Do you understand Now?

So brave with a plan.
Damn, Uncle Dan!

When they didn't believe in me, I knew it was a swindle.
Lost folks in the tall grass?
Oh yes!
EN-EM-IES! HA!

Excuse me, Stephen King.
I was called to tell you about the stranger things.
Closed eyes and bloody noses,
Many won't understand,
So, I never understood what closeness is.

Nothing less than truth,
A legendary message from a chosen kid.

The times are different.
Sunup, sundown.
Day in, Day out.

On the outside looking in,
On the inside but not looking out.
Hopes for a better future,
Or maybe a better picture,
And longing for something more.

Feelings of a best foot forward,
Fears of being smart enough,
and not being smart enough.
Mental battles and deceptions;
learning to overcome them are great lessons,
turned into blessings.

As the wind blows, mysteries unfold
so more stories will be told.

Me.
Everyone else in this wretched world designed –
To corrupt us. End us.
But the best of it is made within us.

Nevertheless, the vacation ahead,
is calling the chosen to begin.

"Do the best you can until you.
know better. Then when you know better,
do better and never let the adversity.
diminish your light."

- Maya Angelou

THE VALLEY

Affliction was my addiction.
That pain would stain me.
Prayers sustained me,
But at times those silver lines overcame me.

What a hole in my soul!
Sad stories never told.
Buried within me, deep down,
Until they overflowed.

Who should I run to?
Who could I run to?

I HAD TO DIG!
I HAD TO CLIMB!

Screaming at my reflection,
"GIRL, STOP WASTING TIME".

I had to gather me,
though there were folks that I loved
who shattered me.

Beautiful Pieces, they were to me.
Astonishingly I became a masterpiece.

I guess in the dark, the light I searched for,
Was myself!

Never give up!
Never stop believing.

Getting out of my way,
Blessed me, and the GOD I'm praying to
protects me.

Life changes.
people changes.
And that's okay.

Out is through.
I fill my tongue with life to you.
What I say is true.

I don't like to make promises;
At times, those tell the difference between
A lie and the truth.

"I was a little theatrical back then…"

- Rosalie Hale

COLD

It's ironic!
You Know?

The winter fell.
Leaves withered up.
The grounds moisture, frozen.

The world is cold.
We are cold.

Hardened hearts.
bad choices.
Not being smart.
Wrecks, death, sickness.
Long hours but no rest,
And still having to fight for what's left.

The world is cold.

Folks see the sleeves you wear,
With your heart on top,
and play it as fettle.
Changing their skin like
The colors in Skittles.

How could a human being's heart?
To them be worth so little?
Who raised you?
Who raised who?

Hard and hardened hearts.
Thoughts gather in my mind

As I gaze, betimes,
at the ice covering highways,
roadways, even the grass upon hills.

I couldn't help but see,
think about the dark souls,
who have lost their will.

I ponder.
I Wander.

Is this how death feels?
Oh, how real!

How must we be absent from love,
From the body,
just to be present with the cold?

No matter if you're young,
don't matter if you're old.
The world is cold.
Dying!

Winter has not come,
Winter has fallen,
And we are cold.

"You go through so
Much shit becoming.
yourself..."

- Anonymous

SURVIVOR

Weak- I need GOD to save me!
All the strength I ever had came from what He gave me.
Walking in the dark looking for his light,
Its bright.

It doesn't matter how wrong you are;
He has the power to make it right.
Make you right.
Took the blind and gave him sight.
He had me winning before I even
knew that I was in a fight.

GOD put us all here to be like Christ.
In his name, there's power,
One youcan you call on at any time.
So real and so truthful ,
His ways are wise,
his character so fruitful,

My prayers, reach out to heaven, saying,
"O father, teach me how to live, teach me how to pray.
Reach deep down in my soul
And take the sins away.

"I'm prolific, so gifted,
I'm the type that's gon' go
get it, No Kiddin'!"

- Nipsey Hussle

A DREAM DESERVED

Have your dreams died?
Were they ever born?
Do your desires cease in an instant?

I couldn't imagine a glimpse of collapse
in divine purpose.
True hunger is as rare as a dire wolf, anew.
It's a rare burning flame,
eternal in all its likeness.

That sudden feeling of discomfort or weakness-
That is hunger.
Not for food, but the ardent desire to persevere.

Who wants to be a crab in the barrel,
Scuffling for crumbs,
or small morsels of meat?

Wake Up!
Yea You!

Hunger comes alive again.
And if you are, stay alive, keep alive.
Be the Hunter.
Who wants to be prey?

There's something precious and specific
about knowing what you are, who you are.
Even when the times change,
or the world changes,
You won't
because you weren't the crab in the barrel.

In fact, you were never in a barrel to begin with.

The truth about life is that it starts with you.
Change your mind.
Change your presentation.
Let your words manifest the wonders
of who you are, what you are.

You are the main character in your life.
So, take charge, OWN THAT!

Don't you ever sit around
and get yourself down.
People are watching more than you think they are.
Hell, they notice things
you would never even think of.

Teach them that it's about you
because you are!
fearfully and wonderfully made.
You're the apple in eyes.
The truth is, you're exactly
who you think you are.

In every era of one's life,
they must be so courageous.
It'd be contagious.
Every room shall be theirs.

Walking with their head held high,
thanking the GOD in the sky
for making them,
taking them on a beautiful journey in life.

No Matter what happens,
Stay consistent.
Stay the course.

Be encouraged, or as they say, "Play the Man",
Which means, walk like GOD
already did it for you.
whatever that may be - take it from me.

Like you're exactly who you want to be,
And where you want to be,
like it's right in front of your eyes.

Live life being okay
with who doesn't choose you,
because you already chose yourself.

Put GOD first.
Be enough for you primarily,
Or you'll be toast - trust me!
Everything else will follow.

Take accountability.
Make no excuses.
DO THIS.
DON'T YOU QUIT!

Because the only way out
is through THIS!
But you Knew this.

You're welcome - you know,
for these gems,
Life is already not easy;
you wouldn't want to be clueless.

"This is never gonna be easy. But in these situations, you gotta guard your heart, guard your mind, guard your spirit. People take, take, take, and that's just the way of the world; nobody ever wants to give anything, but your heart is on your sleeve. You wear it out there, and people see it more than you think they do. And they play on that. Don't end up being a victim all your life. I was for a long time."

– Mary J. Blige

CHOSEN SOLDIERS

Like the air with a cool breeze,

Or "bless you" as one hears a sneeze.

So disciplined,
so eminent with ease,
So different, a light, but an outcast.
Standing out, and built to last,

A truth so loud
one will not have to ask,
Legendary! No need for a pass,

So shamelessly anointed,
Undeserving favor,
Yet favorably appointed.

Just as Moses, blessed with oil,
So pure and without spoil,
Irrevocably rich, roots so deep
As a hill that is steep, even in the dark,

You are blooming out the soil,

Fervent in spirit,
Diligently praying to heaven
That the blood flows instead of boils.

For this call requires more.
Theres no time to be unsure.
This vocation is the core.

Gotta keep blessings coming
as quickly as they are handed,
So, there is no purpose to keeping score.

Deep down in your soul,
Your heart will hold,
the truth that overflows -
For what you are serving for.

A race worth running.
A song worth humming.
Oh, How the Call Has No Withdraw!

Its blameless.
It has no flaw.
Supernatural yet so factual.

Either you win or lose in this race -
There is no draw.

Let not your heart be a hardened,
or grow as cold as theirs.
Oh, may your heart thaw.

Though cries seem hard,
Long and loud,
Detaching from any pain once brought.

Looking back later, Proud!
Understanding for the first time
that it was worth everything it cost.

For every challenge fought,
it was worth beating every Boss.

Wow! What a way to show off.

Could you imagine running
from the snags of the enemy
and never being caught?

HA!
That makes me happier than I thought!

"....That's Major..."

- Young Dolph

ON PURPOSE

Purpose is disruptive.
It's strong like business, head on and bullheaded.
Like blood, but you shed it.
Misunderstood, no matter where you're headed.

What a life! Jesus Christ,
Sounds like heading in the right direction,
offering a distinct perspective,
Not right, not wrong, or corrected.

Some will reject it.
Others will collect it.
But the few that are left
will check it and respect it.

You see, it's the one the world loses.
The world's loss is the universe's greatest gift.

When all the backs are turned,
You feel the wind of the shift.
Don't worry, GOD is not confused.
The world's greatest loss,
But quite the colossal muse.

Oh, so intriguing, lovely, and in tune.
Her fragrance is kind, the songs of her freedom,
It is perfume.

Life is for the living, but a story to the dead.
Legends must have lived –
That way sounds better than said.

Peace and tranquility?
What a lovely cliché.

That little black sheep needed to get away.
Can't sleep at night?
No one to hold you tight?
Ha!
Don't you know that's your soul telling you to pray?

Everything you'll need,
Will be prepared the next day!

So, as volcanoes erupt from the earth,
The same is the world, seeking and seeing your ash,
But pretending that they still must search.

Disruptive. destructive.
But that's only to bring forth some life.
Hiding anointing, in a place full of dying folk,
Well, that just isn't right.

Change is unique.
Being different is okay.
I'd rather be mystique
Then Xavier Charles, anyway.

A voice is a powerful force.
Reminds me of thunder and rain.
You could put the clouds and cold all there,
But it just wouldn't be the same.

Nevertheless, courage, my friend,
That is what you need.
For without courage,

Between destiny and courage,
The promise won't cleave.

Make your adjustments,
Cry if you must, but with everything inside you,
Don't you ever give up.

Disruption is not a curse.
Disruption is a cure.
True love starts from within,
I'm telling you. I'm sure.

Make the necessary moves,
Even if it's that negative attitude.
Keep checking yourself,
You'll never lose.

Forgive yourself!
Hold your head up high!
What a gracious disruption you are -
Fallen from the sky!

"Joy and pain, I like sunshine and rain,"

– Frankie Beverly

SPRING SEASON

Summer air saturated the sun's light as a gift.
All I could think about was joy.
I appreciate the trivial things too.

There I sat humbly and full.
No burdens crept in for the first time.
Leaves fell and flew by like time did,
Though I often dreamt of a timeless world.

"Do what works for you."

- Laura Kennerson

TRUTHS

Life is short – don't abort.
In every aspect, smile.
Be grateful.
Cheer for others; don't be hateful.

Some wouldn't understand,
or even see,
if they had binoculars.

Normalize telling the truth,
even when it isn't popular.

Humility?
Correction?
Why don't we get back to that?

Imagine a world of healing
instead of bleeding –
from lifetime practices of stabbing backs.

Give yourself grace.
Stay away from people and places
that don't respect your space.

There's nothing wrong with working smart or hard
if you don't forget to take a break.

God is real.
You're safe.

If you're searching for common negatives,
you've found the wrong place.

A new year has come upon us.
Please enter it with grace.

For your journey was made selfishly –
desire no other's place.

"Success is a journey, not a destination.
The doing is often more important than the outcome."

- Arthur Ashe

ABOUT THE AUTHOR

C. J. Henry is a passionate writer whose unique style is inspired by the people, experiences, and moments that move her most. Often overlooked in life, she has emerged as an overcomer, refusing to let setbacks, misfortune, or humble beginnings prevent her from turning her dreams into reality. With God at the center of her journey, C. J. Henry seeks to inspire others by proving that determination, faith, and resilience can overcome doubt and adversity.